TO ACT JUSTLY,
LOVE TENDERLY,
WALK HUMBLY

TO ACT JUSTLY, LOVE TENDERLY, WALK HUMBLY

AN AGENDA FOR MINISTERS

Walter Brueggemann
Sharon Parks
Thomas H. Groome

TO ACT JUSTLY, LOVE TENDERLY, WALK HUMBLY

AN AGENDA FOR MINISTERS

Walter Brueggemann
Sharon Parks
Thomas H. Groome

PAULIST PRESS
NEW YORK · MAHWAH

Library of Congress
Catalog Card Number: 85-62877

ISBN: 0-8091-2760-1

Published by Paulist Press
997 Macarthur Boulevard
Mahwah, New Jersey 07430

Printed and bound in the
United States of America

Contents

WALTER BRUEGGEMANN

Preface

New winds are blowing in the church, reshaping its practice of education and pastoral ministry. They blow toward *praxis,* toward faithful action rooted in faithful discernment. They blow toward *spirituality,* aware that the old modes have largely used up their capital and we now lack energy and freedom for the transformation of our faith and the renewal of our common life. New winds are blowing in Scripture study which blow toward *theological commitment,* inviting fresh thought about social criticism and social possibility. As religious education is aware that some old modes have been too domesticated, so in Scripture study it becomes apparent that old critical modes have been excessively "objective," in the wrong ways. It is clear that *praxis and spirituality* in religious education and *theological commitment* in Scripture study are related to each other in important and subtle ways. Together they reflect an awareness among us of the demand and danger that belong to serious faith. Both seek to provide resources and energy to embrace that demand and face that danger.

This book is about that important, subtle relationship. The occasion for this book was a rather remarkable meeting in Portland, Maine in November 1983 under the auspices of Maine Council of Churches. It was the first meeting of its kind in Maine, featuring a new and bold cooperative venture of ecumenical Christianity, including Roman Catholic and Protestant participants. But the important newness of that meeting was the resolve to do ecumenical work on a serious and urgent question, namely the interface between *justice, education,* and *spirituality.* The three papers offered here were the major addresses of the conference. They are published essentially as they were given, so that the informal mode of address in oral presentation has been retained. We believe they warrant further consideration because they speak precisely at the emerging meeting point of *praxis, spirituality, and theological sensitivity.* They may provide the beginnings of a more adequate spirituality to govern the ministry of Church education. Our participation in the conference was important to each of us because across the lines of our disciplines—Scripture study, faith development, and education—we find important points of contact and resonance. We have found it important to think and speak in each other's presence, and we think that it may be so for others. We offer these addresses as a report of our own conversation and as an impetus to further conversation.

The conference had as its theme the text of Micah 6:8, commonly regarded as a focal summary of prophetic faith, prophetic hope and prophetic challenge:

> This is what Yahweh asks of you:
> only this, to act justly,
> to love tenderly,
> and to walk humbly with your God.

It proved to be a rewarding organizing theme. Emerging from the conference was a rich interaction concerning:

1. Scripture study which seeks to move responsibly beyond historical-critical modes;
2. spirituality and its power to renew pastoral-educational

practice by alerting us to the seduction of our cultural situation;

3. prophetic action to which both Scripture and spirituality summon the church;

4. ecumenical cooperation as the indispensable context for faithful action.

It remains for us to thank especially Carl Beyer of the Maine Conference, United Church of Christ, for his vision of the conference and the planning committee which so worked together as to embody the vision the conference sought to teach. Their partnership with us bespeaks the important solidarity between church and academy.

May 4, 1984

WALTER BRUEGGEMANN

Voices of the Night—Against Justice

Micah 6:8 is commonly recognized as a very peculiar and precious summary of the demands of God mediated through the eighth century prophets. In this form, the expectations of God are not general norms (as, for example, natural law) but they are specific expectations placed on God's covenant partner. In this well-known triad of expectations, it is no doubt important that the first element is to *do justice*. In biblical faith, the doing of justice is the primary expectation of God. Everything else by way of ethical norm and covenantal requirement derives from this, for God is indeed a "lover of justice" (Ps 99:4). Israel is here commanded to attend to the very thing which God most values, namely justice.

There are, of course, various and conflicting understandings of justice. Let me offer this as a way the Bible thinks about justice: *Justice is to sort out what belongs to whom, and to return it to them.* Such an understanding implies that there is a right distribution of goods and access to the sources of life. There are certain entitlements which cannot be mocked. Yet through the uneven workings of the historical process, some come to have access to or control of what belongs to others. If we control what belongs to others long enough, we come to think of it as rightly ours, and to forget it belonged to someone else. So the work of liberation, redemption, salvation, is the work of *giving things back*. The Bible knows that when things are alienated from those to whom they belong, there can only be trouble, disorder and death. So God's justice at the outset has a dynamic, transformative quality. It causes things to change, and it expects that things must need change if there is to be abundant life.

I recently heard a story which speaks of forgetting to whom things belong. A very proper lady went to a tea shop. She sat at a table for two, ordered a pot of tea, and prepared to eat some cookies which she had in her purse. Because the tea shop was crowded, a man took the other chair and also ordered tea. As it happened, he was a Jamaican black, though that is not essential to the story. The woman was prepared for a leisurely time, so she began to read her paper. As she did so, she took a cookie from the package. As she read, she noticed that the man across also took a cookie from the package. This upset her greatly, but she ignored it and kept reading. After a while she took another cookie. And so did he. This unnerved her and she glared at the man. While she glared, he reached for the fifth and last cookie, smiled and offered her half of it. She was indignant. She paid her money and left in a great hurry, enraged at such a presumptuous man. She hurried to her bus stop just ouside. She opened her purse to get a coin for her bus ticket. And then she saw, much to her distress, that in her purse was her package of cookies unopened. The lady is not different from all of us. Sometimes we possess things so long that do not really belong to us that we come to think they are ours. Sometimes, by the mercy of God, we have occasion to see to whom these things in fact belong. And when we see that, we have some little chance of being rescued from our misreading of reality. Justice concerns precisely a right reading of social reality, of social power, and of social goods.

I

I begin with some comments about the Micah tradition in the Old Testament. I do this for two reasons. First, because this is the first of three essays, and it seems best to put these things clearly at the outset. Second, because of our different fields of study, I should take responsibility for these more technical matters than my two colleagues who have expertise other than mine.

It is now agreed among a growing number of scholars that Micah is the voice of the village peasant against the rapacious power of the state.[1] That is, Micah needs to be understood in terms of his social context and the social realities in which he is engaged. The peasants watched carefully the growing and shameless power of the Jerusalem government. That urban-scientific-military-industrial establishment had usurped the well-being of the little people. Centralization of power in Jerusalem led to more tightly regimented government intervention, around the predictable agenda of census, taxes and arms. The peasants are always taxed for such state adventurism. And state policies are characteristically a matter of indifference to the peasants, because they will not gain, in any case. So Micah raises the justice question with reference to that social development, the growing power of the urban state. It is worth noting that here as always, the justice question is raised *from below,* not from above. It is implausible that anyone in the Jerusalem circles would raise the justice question, because they are preoccupied with questions of prosperity and security. And they do not notice the cost of prosperity and security imposed on voiceless peasants. In relation to prosperity and security, the establishment regularly thinks that justice questions must be put on hold, or are in any case secondary.

Micah is not simply a free spirit uttering wild charges. Even though his words are in poetry, we can see that he offers a discerning and critical analysis of how in fact it is in this society.[2] The analysis is concerned to establish the profound injustice that is sanctioned and practiced by the dominant order. So the summons to do justice is set in a relentless critique of injustice:

Woe to those who devise wickedness
and work evil upon their beds!
When the morning dawns, they perform it,
because it is in the power of their hand.
They covet fields, and seize them;
and houses, and take them away;
they oppress a man and his house,
a man and his inheritance (2:1-2).

Hear, you heads of Jacob
and rulers of the house of Israel!
Is it not for you to know justice?—
you who hate the good and love the evil,
who tear the skin from off my people,
and their flesh from off their bones...(3:1-2).

Hear this, you heads of the house of Jacob
and rulers of the house of Israel,
who abhor justice
and pervert equity (3:8-9).

Micah names things by their right name. Indeed, that is a primary task of the prophets. There is a systematic perversion of things by calling them by their wrong names, which may be the supreme achievement of "1984" (cf. Is 5:20). It is a hard and precious gain when things get identified for what they are.

Of these indictments from Micah, we may note three important factors. First, the poetry is *addressed to the leadership,* to the ones with social power. They are the ones who have arranged things the way they are. They are also the ones who benefit from the way things are. Second, the agenda is consistently *economic.* The real issues concerning justice have to do with access to and control of life-goods. We have so much to learn yet about this as the proper agenda of the Bible, and indeed as the proper agenda of God. That agenda has been on God's mind since the exodus. Third, address to leadership and concern for economics make clear that Micah is making a *critique of the system* of social control. This is not poetry that simply strikes out at a specific act. It is a much more sustained analysis based on the legal precedent of the torah to show that the entire social system is wrongly directed. So the invitation to do justice is in a context of *the systemic power of evil.*

Now it is not very difficult to see the parallels between Micah's social context and ours. Now, as then, we live in a set of power relations where some folks do not have what belongs to them, precisely because others have, use and enjoy what is not theirs. And we are like the woman in the tea shop. We notice late and with regret that what we were eating and enjoying in fact belongs to someone else.

The implications for education are enormous. By and large, Christian thought in America, indeed American social awareness generally, is uninformed and innocent. So I suggest that an important educational task, with both adults and children, is to provide some of the awarenesses and tools for social criticism so that we may begin to think systemically both about the *distortions* that do us in, and the *alternatives* that are resonant with our faith. Unless we are equipped for such social analysis, we end up with occasional and isolated acts of social indignation but without the power or imagination for the long haul, which is necessary if there is to be serious social transformation.

II

In that context, Micah proposes a radical alternative for the ordering of society.

It shall come to pass in the latter days
    that the mountain of the house of the Lord

shall be established as the highest of the mountains,
    and shall be raised up above the hills;
and peoples shall flow to it,
    and many nations shall come, and say:
"Come, let us go up to the mountain of the Lord,
    to the house of the God of Jacob;
that he may teach us his ways
    and we may walk in his paths."
For out of Zion shall go forth the law,
    and the word of the Lord from Jerusalem.
He shall judge between many peoples,
    and shall decide for strong nations afar off;
and they shall beat their swords into plowshares,
    and their spears into pruning hooks;
nation shall not lift up sword against nation,
    neither shall they learn war any more;
But they shall sit every man under his vine and under his
    fig tree, and none shall make them afraid;
for the mouth of the Lord of hosts has spoken(4:1-4).

This is a remarkable scenario, which envisions a complete reordering of international power. Micah offers a vision of the nations submitting to the torah of Yahweh. And when that submission has been made, there can be disarmament. And when there is genuine disarmament, some will not have what rightly belongs to another. Disarmament is not a commitment in a vacuum, but is part of the justice-making process. The other side of the issue, in this poem, is the willingness to settle for a peasant standard of living, content with vine and fig tree.[3] So peace envisioned here requires a shift of economic priorities, which permits the end of greed, the end of rapacious taxes, the end of exploitation either by strong parties or by ruthless governments.

The poem envisions a changed social system. But it also presumes a changed set of social priorities and social appetites.

It anticipates nothing less than the dismantling of the presently-known world for the sake of an alternative world not yet embodied. This poem is a part of Micah's vision of justice[4] to which our text enjoins us. The justice of which Micah speaks requires two elements:

a) A *firm and clear critique* of what is going on. Micah sees clearly that what is going on is the rapaciousness of the strong against the weak, all in the name of the war system. Micah does not flinch. But we may also be sure that in his time, or in ours, such a massive critique will be mightily resisted.

b) A *poetic scenario of an alternative way* to order society around the gifts of God. Indignant liberals are often stronger on the first than the second. But it is this act of liberated hope that gives credibility to the critique. For unless there is an alternative around which to rally, then one should not knock the only game in town. But the poetry of 4:1-4 asserts that the present way is not the only game in town. Prophetic faith invites Israel to an alternative.

Thus, Micah's program of poetry may be a guide for our ways in education. To do justly requires both *critique and alternative.*

- Economically: Micah contrasts a mode of life in which everything is possessed and a world in which gifts are freely given.
- Epistemologically: Micah breaks from the fixed world of tightly controlled memos. In their place he offers poetry. For those who live best in a world of memos which control, po-

• Linguistically:

etry does not seem very efficient. But that, of course, is the point. Justice will not come in a society that is excessively efficient, so that even the mode of knowing offers a challenge. Micah offers a story (cf. 6:3-5 on the exodus) that is a tale to be followed, as an alternative to a management scheme. The story seems too peculiar, and scandalously particular. One cannot mount from it a massive imperial program. But of course, that is exactly what the poet has in mind, that the truth by which to live is made available only in odd break points, in the seams between our managed reality.

We are now prepared to turn to our text. In doing so, I hope these comments have prepared the way. Micah is a watchful peasant who sees the great and irresistible power of the state, chewing away at the life-stuff of his people. And he insists, by the mercy of God, that such a way of ordering reality is false and does not need to be, and, in the end, cannot prevail against God's justice that attends to the voiceless peasant.

III

The text of 6:1-8 (of which our verse is the conclusion) is commonly regarded as a law-suit, in which Israel and Yahweh have come to court to see which one is at fault in this fractured relationship.[5] The premise of the poem is that something is profoundly amiss.

1. Vv. 3-5 are an historical review that takes Israel back in imagination to the moments of origin. The crucial trio of Moses, Aaron and Miriam are named, and the memory moves

on to the earliest form of land-taking. In this short space, the entire early history of Israel is referenced, from leaving *Egypt* to the coming into the *land of promise.* The whole is reference to "the saving acts of the Lord" (v. 5) which in Hebrew speaks of the way in which God has made things *right.* The poem offers to Israel a *memory of redemption.* Israel recalls here that its origins are in *helplessness,* when Israel could do nothing against superior power. And in the face of that helplessness came the miracle of God's liberating *graciousness.* The moment of origin was a peculiar match *between Israel's helplessness* and *God's graciousness* which had the power to liberate and make new.

Education for justice has to do with returning to such a season of origin. None of us, nor all of us together, was born strong. Our birthing as persons and as community was a birthing into weakness, vulnerability and need. Along the way, we have established other definitions of self-deception which tease us into thinking about our strength (cf. Dt 8:17). And when we think of our strength, we have inordinate imaginations and we forget the gift of life in that originary moment which we had no power to generate. Our excessively personalistic education has caused us to neglect the model available to us here, that our origin is in a season of inexplicable gift.

2. It is such an embarrassingly long move from vv. 3-5 to vv. 6-7. Now it is as though the memory has been completely wiped out. Israel remembers nothing, but tries to come at God (and no doubt the neighbor) from a posture of strength. This is a strange speech of bargaining, in which the worshiper wants to come to the throne of God with the least price available. Micah 3:11 mentions bribes in human interaction. Here the bribery is with God. Many commentators have noted that in these two verses, there is an ascending order of value which runs from *calves* through *rams* to *rivers of oil* and finally to *first-born son,* the most prized "possession" available.

How dare one think about such a buy-off of God! Well, one dares, if one has forgotten the exodus memory. Then everything can be reduced to a commodity. Even one's treasured son can become a bargaining chip. Because nothing really has any intrinsic value. All valuing has been lost when the originary story is forfeited.

So the substance of vv. 6-7 stands in wondrous contrast to that of vv. 3-5. Indeed, they articulate two different notions of justice. The exodus memory speaks of gift and redemption, of gratitude, self-giving and self-commitment. The questions of bidding in vv. 6-7 speak of bargaining and calculation. How one stands on these issues is decisive for the ways in which justice is understood.

The contrast between the two is echoed, I suggest, in the narrative of Jesus observing temple offerings (Lk 21:1-4). On the one hand, there is a rich man who gives out of "his abundance." On the other hand, there is a poor widow who gives out of her "poverty." She "put in all the living that she had." It is like that in our text. Vv. 3-5 invite people in touch with the memory to come *out of their poverty,* mindful that it is all gift. But the vigorous questions of vv. 6-7 sound like one in *abundance* who has plenty and will share it with God. It need hardly be said, does it, that the issue put this way is congruent with the problem we abundant ones face in thinking through and deciding about justice. And finally how we think about justice in the world depends on how we understand ourselves, our position in life, our rootage, our shaping memories.

IV

Finally, we come to our verse. The three elements are well known to us. To do justice, to love kindness, to walk humbly with God—these may embody all that we need to know in order to be faithful and to be human. They are not three "virtues." They are not three "things to do." Rather, they speak of three dimensions of a life of faithfulness, each of which depends on and is reinforced by the other two. To *love kindness (hesed)* means to enter into relationships of abiding solidarity. It means to make commitments and to keep commitments. And so the questions come: With whom? And in what way? The New Testament struggles with the question of the limits of solidarity. In Luke 10:29, the neighbor question is the overriding question for the community, as it still is. And in what way to do kindness? We learn how to practice solidarity by discerning the ways in which God practices solidarity. The biblical story is the account of God's resilient solidarity. That is why one must *walk humbly with God.* The phrase is marvelously ambiguous. The more obvious reading is that because God is so powerful, in God's presence we must be humble. But one can also read that God's own walk is humble, and so if one would walk the way of God, one must also walk humbly. So the solidarity of God's *hesed* is not a powerful, overriding solidarity, but it is a patient, attentive, waiting, hoping solidarity.

But God's solidarity *(hesed)* is not just an act of humble solidarity. It is also an active intervention that changes things. So one is enjoined to *do justice,* as God does justice. And when God does justice, it is not modest or polite or understated. It is an act of powerful intervention. It is like Moses in the court of Pharaoh insisting on freedom. It is like Nathan sent to David (2 Sam 12) who will not tolerate such rapacious action. It is like Elijah thundering against Ahab and Jezebel when Naboth has been done in, for the sake of land (I Kgs 21). God is a lover of justice, which means God intervenes for the poor and weak against the powerful who have too much (Ps 99:4). And so Israel is enjoined to love the marginal in justice-working ways, precisely because that is how God works (cf. Dt 10:18-19). What can be readily noticed is that justice is no holding action in order to maintain equilibrium. It is rather an active intervention aimed at transformation of social power. And this is derivative from Micah's understanding of God which is interventionist. *To do justice:* To sort out what belongs to whom, and to return it to them. In this prophetic tradition, justice presumes *social entitlements.* These entitlements are not based in natural law or in created order, but in the initial acts of Israel's historical memory. Israel has a social vision in which every family, clan and tribe has its rightful place of power.[6] Where these entitlements are fully honored, there is justice, assuring each the power for life, access to public decisions, fair treatment in court. Where the entitlements are distorted or usurped, there is injustice against which powerful intervention must be made.

In Micah's day, as in ours, the entitlements of the rural have a hard time against urban bureaucracy. The economically marginal have a difficult time against the urban elite. Simple disconnected folk have an impossible time against large aggregates of power. So in that society (as in our society) the agents of government (especially the king as in Psalm 72) are called to be *agents of justice against every social distortion.*

Justice then is not a romantic social ideal for another world. It is the hard work of redeploying social power and the transformation of the social system. It includes:

a) *The reality of social entitlement* which no amount of social monopoly can ever legitimately nullify. This is why Israel prohibits moving ancient boundary markers (Dt 19:14). They protect the weak against usurpation.

b) The periodic *cancellation of debts* which is at the heart of the Jubilee Year institution (Lev 25). This is an odd social notion that the vicious cycle must be broken. What debt cancellation does is permit the failed ones to resume their place of respect, power and dignity in the community. Every society is based on indebtedness, to see who owes

what to whom. Biblical talk of forgiveness concerns the
end of that form of social control, to let folk be free in each
other's presence.[7]

c) *Redistribution of land* (as envisioned in Micah 2:1-5) is
the supreme measure of justice. It is worth noting that the
bloodiest social conflicts in our time (in the Near East and
in Central America) have to do with land monopoly and
land reform. We may imagine that in an increasingly
money-orientated society, land does not hold such a crucial position. But the evidence is that the reality is still
central.

All three elements—entitlement, debt cancellation and land
redistribution—mean to disrupt and dismantle the present
ordering of things, because the present order is seen to be
unjust. It should be obvious that we here are at the center of
the radicalness of biblical faith.

Now one must think carefully what this means for Church
education. In our society, educational programs are not likely
to undertake the practice of such policy. But more modest jobs
can be done which serve the cause of justice. I believe there is
much need to "redescribe the world" so that it can be seen in
these categories. And those of us who benefit from the inequal-
ity in the world have incredible blind spots and will struggle to
keep those spots blind. But one must conclude from Micah and
the whole tradition that *the redistribution of social power* is a
crucial element of the Gospel. And that is the summons of
justice.

I can think of three levels of responsibility, all of which
need to be addressed:

a) There are *theological issues* involved here. Specifically, we
need a careful rethinking of who God is. It is the case that
functionally the God of Church gets presented as an ally of

those who have a monopoly on social power. Indeed, our conventional, uncritical understanding of God is that God has all power and all knowledge. So God is the natural companion of human agencies which also possess power and knowledge. We have much work to do on our understanding of God if we are to have a theological basis from which to think through the doing of justice. I suggest Psalm 82 to be a most crucial beginning point for such work, because there it is affirmed that God's godness consists in solidarity with the marginal against those, human or divine, who only care about self.

b) Clearly we have, if we care about doing justice, to address matters of *policy formation*. Social justice does not come from good intentions or noble theology but from the development of social policy which will change the distribution of power and goods, as well as access to political decision-making. This is not a matter upon which I will comment, as I want to move on to another area which I judge to be even more pressing for Church education.

c) The third area I identify in relation to doing justice concerns *attending to "the voices of the night."* I refer to reasonable action, such as policy formation, as "daytime work." But that daytime work will not have great staying power unless it is accompanied by pastoral attention to the power of unreason that pervades and often shapes our common life. I submit that it is the peculiar work of the Church to address these matters, because the Church has access to these aspects of life like no one else in our society. That work can be undertaken pastorally, educationally and liturgically. Indeed, I have come to think that this unreasonable dimension of human agenda is the focus of the prophets we have under study. They did not propose policy matters, but they addressed the issues of human speech, human fear, human hope, human perception, all of which lie underneath and are determinative of social policy.

V

So I want to consider the doing of justice in the presence of unresolved "voices of the night."[8] I offer two examples: First, on October 4, 1983, in Huntsville, Texas, James D. Autry was to die by injection, at the sentence of the state. At the last minute, Justice Byron White granted a stay of execution. Preparation for the execution had advanced so far that Autry already had tubes in his arms to carry the lethal poison when the action was cancelled.

What is stunning is that (as Anthony Lewis reports)[9] "a crowd of people shouted for his death whenever television lights were turned on." "Kill him, kill him, kill him," they chanted. I do not want to comment on the state execution. I focus on the crowd reaction which reflects an unresolved vengeance and a thirst for blood of an utterly unreasonable kind.

Second, a friend of mine has begun to study theology. She is a bright, teachable, middle-class liberal. Her husband is an engineer, one of the best in the nation at what he does. But when he got a whiff of what we teach in seminary, with a little reading on the subject, he became enraged, wanted to correct things, wanted to leave the Church. Until that moment, though a practicing Church member, he had not a serious clue about the transformative scandal which is the Gospel. His response was all *quid pro quo* and work ethic based on deep fear. His response, I suggest, is yet another evidence of "the voice of the night" that lives among us all.

The data need not be multiplied. I add only that the late "open line" radio program each night in my city reveals an incredible amount of unreason, hatred and violence that waits for satisfaction. And I think it not a far move from that to the crazy commitment we have to more and more arms. For I judge that such arms production and deployment cannot be justified by reasonable policy, but only by the unresolved and undisciplined exaggerations of the nighttime. The voices of the night include the voice of greed, the voice of having made it, the voice of fear. All these voices are arraigned against the prophetic summons to justice. Church educators must acknowledge, receive and deal with this unreason if we are ever to be free for the real task of justice.

VI

The educational task of the Church includes honoring, taking seriously and processing the voices of the night to the agenda of justice. We have characterized justice as the practice of *entitlement* for the weak and incompetent. So our task is to bring such frightened persons and indeed frightened system to the practice of entitlement. And that is most difficult for all of us, for in fact entitlement, for those who have not, is against our presumed vested interest.

This nurture task that will permit justice is complicated and difficult. It must be based in communion with the vulnerable God (who walks humbly) and in openness to neighbor acts of kindness *(hesed)*. But the unreason militates against both. The unreason which is personal and common does not want or countenance a vulnerable God who walks humbly, and does not much value neighbor acts of solidarity.

The truth is that in our society most of us have a disproportion of social goods and social power. And we fear the loss of our disproportion. We do not ask how we got it or what it does to others. We are, in middle America, convinced that the "system is the solution." By this, we mean that the present practice of "consumer militarism" serves well some of us who benefit from the stacking of the cards. In fact, we mean to say that we like the system because it preserves and legitimates the present disproportion which is in our favor. And here in this text (as in the Bible generally) we are invited to justice which means to reverse the disproportion. To hold to the disproportion or to reverse the disproportion is the issue of justice. And when we become defensive about that, we are driven in our unreasonableness to vengeance. So I submit that in order to work at peace in a serious way in our culture, Church educators must reckon with the deep and broadly based thirst for vengeance which lies invisible, but which powers and legitimates our policies of injustice.

1. Vengeance precludes justice. Vengeance acts out of rage, a need to hurt. But vengeance then is not an irrational act. It is driven by an irrationality, but acts in ways the world can call rational. There is a calculation in its implementation. And in our situation in American culture, one has the impression that vengeance serves to defend "the system," to strike out at those who upset the system. This kind of vengeance is a practice of those who benefit from the system, who are not blind to their own self-interest, but who mask it in ways of legitimacy.

2. I judge that we are so much a community of vengeance because we have so much to defend. We have in the world a disproportion of social goods and social power. And we label those who challenge that disproportion as "thugs." But we seem not to notice that our own actions are equally "thuggish," only in the interest of our disproportion. So we bomb a Grenadan hospital and write it off as a "mistake." Those of us with so much to defend (and that includes most of us) are not good candidates for justice. And yet that is our educational mission.

3. Helping people handle and process vengeance in healthy ways is an overriding task. The vengeance which surfaces in the night, but which hurts in reasonable ways in the daylight, is deep in our social fabric. But it is not disinterested. And so the interest must be exposed, so that we may begin to sort out what our true interest is, and what our presumed, mistaken interest is. I suggest there are only three ways this deep night-filled vengeance can be handled:

(a) It can be *acted out*. For those who have means to do so, this may take the form of terror. But for those who would never resort to terror in the streets, it can be acted out either in terms of deathly policies (against the poor), or, closer to home, it can evidence itself in terms of abuse against those whom we love, as in wife abuse and child abuse. Something must be done with the passions of the night and one way is to act on them.

(b) A second way, our best way, given our socio-economic place, is to *deny* that we are so. The practice of repression is deep in our society and no doubt some repression makes it possible for us to live together. But we do know, in our nights of honesty, that even the repressed darkness will have its say, one way or another.

(c) The third way of handling this passion of the night is to submit it to the sovereign will of God. This can be done in liturgical, pastoral, educational ways. It may happen best in symbolic, nearly sacramental acts which require both a robust God and an honest community which is stable and open enough to permit such processing.

4. The processing of vengeance may involve at least the following:[10]

(a) An acknowledgement that God is a God of vengeance and justice. Vengeance cannot be handled by a trivial, romantic God, but only by one who is offended at injustice and who takes seriously the wrongs done against us or our fellows.

(b) As repression requires silence, so the processing of vengeance requires speech, honest and full. One must bring the anger and resentment to *articulation,* but it must be done in a context where one can take responsibility for what one says.

(c) When such passions are fully articulated, they can also be *submitted* to God. The most difficult thing to entrust to God is not our fault, but our rage, anger and hatred when we have been wronged. To submit such matters to God means to be able to trust God with our most precious dimension. It requires trust in God to submit to God and leave it there for God's resolve. It is an act of trust that God will act seriously. Now it follows that this entrustment of God is risky for two reasons. First, though we are sure God will act, God may not act on it in our way. God's action may seem to us not forceful enough, not quick enough, not severe enough. But leaving it with God is to let God do things in a "more excellent way." Second, this entrustment means that we may not take it back from God. We cannot later change our minds and recover our darkness off God's desk. When it is articulated and submitted, this is an irreversible act of relinquishment.

(d) There is an outcome to the process of *articulation, submission* and *relinquishment.* It is that we are liberated. We are freed to move on, to take on other issues in healthy ways. Now it is my judgment that when we have been helped by our community through the process of articulation, submission and relinquishment, we are freed enough to do justice. My growing impression, however, is that unless this nighttime work with the passions of vengeance is done well and intentionally, we shall never be free enough for the important daytime work of policy formation, constituency development, and planning for actions of social transformation. While many agents may address the work of the daytime, the work with the passions of the night is more difficult and in our society is peculiarly entrusted to the pastors and educators of the Church.

VII

Making a move toward Micah's summons to justice, kindness, humbleness with God requires *an extrication from the system of disproportion.* That extrication requires intellectual, emotional and economic imagination. It requires that we should be able to envision ourselves differently from the way the world defines us. It is a complicated and difficult act, and we resist it greatly. I am convinced that such an extrication begins as a liturgical, pastoral event. I conclude with comments on the doxology in Micah 7:18-20, which concludes the poetic collection of Micah.

1. Whereas Micah 6:8 is essentially a summons, this is a doxology. This is the beginning point, for our transformation on earth depends on our acknowledgment that things have been decisively altered in heaven, among the gods. So this is a statement about the reality and distinctiveness of God. And the key factor is that God is one who forgives, who breaks the vicious cycles and who allows for a beginning again.

Attention may be called to three words about God. In v. 18, this God delights in *steadfast love* (our same word *hesed*).[11] This God delights in acts of solidarity. In v. 19, God is marked by womb-like *compassion,* a readiness to put behind all the scars and hurts that have marred the relationship. And in v. 20, this God is marked by *faithfulness* to promises, an assurance that the old promises of new life are the overriding reality for the community in any time and circumstance. This characterization of God is a platform for our doing of justice. This is not the God we expected to see, nor the God mostly assumed in our culture. That god, that false god, is more often marked by omnipresence, omnipotence, omniscience. Such a god never permits a beginning again, because all the fractures are held in the balance to perpetuity. And then justice cannot happen. But the God of this poem, the one marked by *steadfast love, compassion, faithfulness (hesed, raham, 'emeth)* is a God who makes justice possible, because there is a beginning again.

2. The beginning of justice requires a new discernment of who God is. The educators of the Church must be theologically intentional, because everything follows from our discernment of God. This "new God" (cf. Jdt 5:8) breaks with imperial modes of reality which sanction injustice in the name of order. This "new God" celebrates new folk. This new God is an embodiment of the action of submission and relinquishment which we are invited to replicate in our social life.

3. The promise of God in Micah 7:20 is an anticipation of the poetry of Mary in Luke 1:46-55. There, also, the poem is rooted in the Abrahamic memory and promise. The song of Mary is remarkably and abrasively about an inversion that will permit justice:

> He has put down the mighty from their thrones,
> and exalted those of low degree;
> He has filled the hungry with good things,
> the rich he has sent empty away (vv. 52-53).

How odd and how energizing that this poem of Mary stands at the center of our liturgical memory. It is one way in which the summons to justice is enacted among the marginal.

4. Justice finally is about inversion, about the difficult

adjustment of the disproportion. It is about a God who inverts, as God did in the exodus from the empire. It is about a neighbor who waits desperately for an inversion. But neither the readiness of God nor the needfulness of the neighbor is enough. I suspect that the doing of justice requires that the strong, vengeful one (who could be almost any of us in our society) must finally touch his or her own pain. It is when we touch our pain that we begin to notice the pain of others and the ways in which our system generates and requires such pain. It is in the awareness of our own pain, not unlike the pain of the others, that "the song of the underneath" begins to be our song. And as we sing this song from underneath, we take on new energy for the prophetic summons. It can happen that when we sing our pain, the song of pain can be extended and we begin to notice the others who are hurt, sometimes even by us.

And when that singing can include the others who are fellow sufferers and often our victims, the voices of the night lose their terror and their power over us. When the song has reached the heart of the pain and lingered there, it can be changed into a new song. It cannot be changed easily or lightly, but only by entering the pain. But when it happens, then policies for justice, for entitlement, for redressing the disproportion, can be formed. Then the crowd no longer chants "kill, kill, kill," but may turn to forgiveness. And someday somewhere at a bus stop when we find our package of cookies unopened in our purse, we may realize we have been eating cookies that belong to another. We may smile in gratitude, free of resentment, and resolve to share our own.

Such a transformation is healing and joyous. But it is not romantic. It requires of us that we face fully the disproportion that needs to be acknowledged, submitted and relinquished. Prophetic faith holds out the insistent hope that people like us can make such a move. Church educators stand at the place where the transformative summons gets underway.

Notes

1. See most importantly Hans Walter Wolff, "Micah the Moreshite—The Prophet and His Background," *Israelite Wisdom,* ed. by John G. Gammie (Missoula, Montana: Scholars Press, 1978) 77-84, and his more extended discussion of the same issues in "Wie verstand Micha von Moreshet sein prophetisches Amt?" SVT 29 (1977) 403-17. Less directly see also Bernhard Lang, "The Social Organization of Peasant Poverty in Biblical Israel," JSOT 24 (1982) 47-63, and Robert Coote, *Amos Among the Prophets* (Philadelphia: Fortress Press, 1981) 24-42.

2. On the social location of prophecy, and especially Micah, see the definitive statement by Robert R. Wilson. *Prophecy and Society in Ancient Israel* (Philadelphia: Fortress Press, 1980) 272-74 and *passim.*

3. On this text, see my analysis, "Vine and Fig Tree: A Case Study in Imagination and Criticism," CBQ 43 (1981)188-204.

4. On this theme, see James L. Mays, "Justice: Perspectives from the Prophetic Tradition," *Interpretation* 37 (1983) 5-17.

5. On this text, among the important dicussions are: Elizabeth Achtemier, "How To Stay Alive," Micah 6:8, *Theology and Life 6* (1963) 275-82; John Calvin, "Calvin's Saturday Sermon on Micah 6:6-8," SJT 23 (1970) 166-82; Phillip Hyatt, "On the Meaning and Origin of Micah 6:8," ATR 34 (1952) 332-39; T. Lescow, "Micah 6:6-8: Studien zu Sprache, Form und Auslegung" (Stuttgart: Calwer Verlag, 1966). I am indebted to my colleague, John Bracke, for some of these references.

6. The "egalitarian revolution" which constitutes the Israelite vision of social reality has been given classic formulation by Norman K. Gottwald, *The Tribes of Yahweh* (Maryknoll, N.Y.: Orbis Books, 1979).

7. On forgiveness as a social reality, see Patrick D. Miller, Jr., "Luke 4:16-21," *Interpretation* 29 (1975) 417-21.

8. See Brueggemann, "Reservoirs of Unreason," *Reformed Liturgy and Music* 17 (1983) 99-104.

9. Anthony Lewis, "Kill Him, Kill Him, Kill Him, Kill Him," *Post-Dispatch* (Oct. 16, 1983).

10. See my discussion of this matter as it relates to the liturgic life of the Psalms, *Praying the Psalms* (Winona, Minn.: St. Mary's Press, 1982) chapter 5.

11. On *hesed* and acts of solidarity, see Katharine Sakenfeld, *The Meaning of Hesed* in the Hebrew Bible (Missoula, Montana: Scholars Press, 1978) and her book *Faithfulness in Action; Loyalty in Biblical Perspective* (Philadelphia: Fortress Press, 1985).

SHARON PARKS

...Love Tenderly...

We have turned aside, you and I, from the people, places, and projects that might have claimed this time to reflect on the question: What does God ask of us?

In these last days, the attack on our marines in Beirut and our attack on Grenada have confronted us anew with the terror of our vulnerability and the scope of our power. As our psyches are bludgeoned and our consciences are buffeted into a renewed uneasiness, we gather in this place to ask: What does God ask of us? In our questioning we turn to our tradition, the ancient, distilled wisdom of our people's seeking and being sought by God, and we read in the Jerusalem Bible,

> This is what Yahweh asks of you:
> only this, to act justly,
> to love tenderly,
> and to walk humbly with your God.

I have been invited to guide our reflection upon the admonition "to love tenderly." I would like to begin to do so by sharing a true story of a six year old girl.

This little girl was being tucked into bed in another in a much too long line of foster homes by yet one more temporary "mother." The new foster mother was surprised when the little girl asked her to take off her wedding ring so she could see it. But wanting to respond warmly to the little girl, she did

29

as requested, and then was startled when the little girl clutched the ring tightly and putting her little fist firmly under her pillow she said, "There. Now you won't leave me while I'm sleeping."[1]

I invite us as educators concerned with the formation of faith to recognize that the central issues of faith were at stake for that little girl—belief and doubt, promise and betrayal, power and powerlessness, belonging and exclusion, suffering and hope. That little girl represents the dialectic of faith—and not just because she is a child. She knew that ring to be precious to the adult, primarily because of its power to touch the adult experience of belief and doubt, promise and betrayal, power and powerlessness, belonging and exclusion, suffering and hope.

But in a single action, this little girl reveals not only the dialectic of faith but also a profound vulnerability. Faith and vulnerability are not polar opposites but are integral to each other. Thus if you and I are to nurture the life of faith, we cannot do so without attention to the inherent vulnerability of "faithing" persons—we must love tenderly.

I was asked to lead our reflection on this phrase "to love tenderly" in part because the leadership of this conference perceived a connection between the call "to love tenderly" and the emerging inter-disciplinary study termed faith development in which I am engaged.[2] Their perception is, I believe, accurate. To love tenderly is to love with an awareness of the capacity of the other to be wounded, to suffer pain, and to be dependent upon relationship with others. To love tenderly requires a particular capacity of spirit and an informed sensitivity. Faith development theory offers a perspective that can assist us in orienting an understanding which calls forth compassion.

This theoretical perspective, which sets in dialogue insights from theology and developmental psychology, helps to illumine the particular character of each era in the human life span and contributes to an informed understanding of the dynamics of transition in the journey of faith. As such, this theoretical lens has a significant power to describe the underlying, creative strength of the soul manifest in the dynamics of healing, growth, and transformation. But this perspective also has power to inform aspects of human vulnerability. This second power is essential to any psychology, theology, or educational theory which must serve a culture that overvalues the virtues of autonomy, the strength to stand alone and the capacity to act independently. The creation of a positive human future requires frames of reference which not only describe individual strength but also compel attention to the virtues of dependence, inter-dependence, and the capacity to be vulnerable.

I suggest that there are three important dimensions of human vulnerability that faith development brings into focus. First, this theoretical perspective reminds us that faith is not a matter of mere cognition divorced from feeling. Faith is a dynamic phenomenon manifested in emotion, as well as in cognition. Faith involves the whole of a person's being. In common discourse the word "faith" has come to mean to many something like mere intellectual assent to abstract propositions or dogma; however, in faith the rational and the passional are fused.[3] Wilfred Smith has helped us see that in its original usage the word faith connoted the activity of setting one's heart, of holding dear, of honoring, of trusting. As such faith is cognitive and affective and not only a noun, but also a verb— and an activity in which all human beings are engaged.[4]

William F. Lynch, a Jesuit, helps us to reimage faith in this way by describing faith as a primal, elemental force within the human, demanding order out of chaos. He imagines faith as coming into force in the womb.[5] Here we can imagine that at the very dawn of human awareness there is a rudimentary sense of relation, of wholeness, and a sense of an ultimate environment that intends our good. Then in the experience we call birth, one undergoes what must be experienced as utter chaos—sound louder than ever before, light, touch, breathing. And the task of faith is then to compose that which was promised at the dawn of existence, to compose a trustworthy ultimacy.

Erik Erikson describes the first task of human being as the establishment of "basic trust."[6] In the way of seeing suggested here, we may think of the first task of human being as the *re*-establishment of basic trust. But we know that this does not happen, if at all, merely once and for all. Rather the journey of faith requires that over and over again we undergo the coming apart and recomposing of our most cherished patterns of meaning and anchors of trust.

Our vocation as educators is to lead out in this journey of faith, to nurture an on-going process of transformation, and to care for the adequacy of its formulations (the theological dimension of our task). We cannot do so without recognizing the courage and cost required for growth in faith. To undergo the loss of one's fundamental but finite understandings of Truth, to let go of grounding assumptions of self, world, and God, is to enter into feelings of anxiety and doubt and to experience the unraveling or rending of the very fabric of life. The transformation of faith is only occasionally precipitated by intellectual inquiry, and rather more frequently occurs in the midst of the experience of the defeat of our assumptions and dreams—illness, loss of relationship, collision with the limits of one's own power and competence, betrayal by the expected forms of public life. Though we discover a more adequate faith beyond the broken forms of an earlier faith, it costs. To move through such experience requires courage of the strongest sort. In the process a person is vulnerable to the temptation to build defenses against the loss of faith and meaning. Such defenses may subsequently burden, distort and maim the ongoing journey of life. Therefore, the pilgrimage of faith must be made in the company of others. To tolerate the vulnerability required for the formation of a more adequate faith requires the presence of a supportive, nurturing environment. Jean Piaget, the grandfather of constructive-developmental psychology, described the development of the underlying structures of knowing so as to recognize that the development of cognition depends upon an interaction between the person and the environment. A person develops increasingly complex structures of cognition in the presence of stimuli which challenge without overwhelming the present structures. Robert Kegan, representing a neo-Piagetian perspective, extends Piaget's insight beyond a focus on cognition, describing this constructive-developmental activity as the central activity of personality, that is, not only cognition but the whole person is formed and transformed in the inter-action of person and environment. Thus educators cannot focus on persons alone, for growth is dependent upon the quality of the whole environment. Human faith is shaped, not only by the activity of faith within (as some notions of spirituality or piety might suggest), but also by inter-action with others in the world.

Indeed, as human beings we seem to be dependent upon a *network of belonging,* or "those who count."[7] We require a sense of connection with others who confirm our being and provide a "home" which grounds or secures our sense of personal and corporate well-being. Such a network of belonging may take the form of an identifiable group located in a single geographical place, or may it be dispersed geographically, or it may be only one other individual being (living or dead), but whatever the form, we are dependent upon that belonging and vulnerable to its limits and its loss.

This dynamic is one to which the educator must give

particularly sensitive attention when faith is in transition. Kegan, drawing on the insight of Winnicott, asserts that a "holding environment" is essential to development.[8] When one's faith and self come apart to come together again, there must be a supporting, nurturing environment that "holds" us.

The need for such a holding environment in infancy and early childhood is generally understood, but the holding capacity of the environment is of critical importance in later eras as well. I have a friend who had a nurturing family and a happy childhood through her early school years. When she went to junior high, however, a very troubled girl managed to torment her and for a time succeeded in alienating her from the rest of the peer group. The situation became so severe that the only way that caring parents and her teacher felt they could assist was to allow her not to attend school for a period. In time the loyalties of the group shifted and she was again included; but scars remain and are manifest in a deeply felt anxiety she experiences whenever she comes to a new threshold which invites her to step into an enlarged area of becoming—even when the new possibilities are attractive to her and she knows at a rational level that she is competent to respond. For when she was at a time of one of life's major transitions, puberty, her primary social environment failed to hold so as to carry her across that threshold.

Her parents and teacher were by that time a necessary but no longer sufficient part of her holding environment; the adolescent requires, for the first time, his or her own "autonomous" relationship with the larger social world. There is a sense in which the adolescent is as dependent as the infant upon persons "out there" to welcome one into larger being. The fragile character of the untested social expansion of the young adolescent asks for support and protection; it is the vocation of church youth groups, schools and other forms of community care to respond to this need. Though most poi-

gnantly vivid in infancy and early adolescence, this need for a
holding environment is present throughout the life span. If we
are to learn and to grow, we need an environment that will be,
at least in part, tender with us. Do the educational contexts
which we create serve as holding environments for children,
adolescents—and adults?

The primary educational environment in which I teach
and learn is Harvard University. The environment may be
characterized, in part, by such words as challenging, rigorous,
critical and competitive. At the beginning of the last Lenten
season, Krister Stendahl presided at the Ash Wednesday service in the chapel of the Divinity School. There at the threshold
of a new season in liturgical time, time set aside to be unlike
other time, he offered us a wonderful gift. He read from the
103rd Psalm: "As a parent is tender to the children, so the Holy
One is tender...for God knows our frame and remembers that
we are dust." And so he urged us to be tender toward one
another during the forty days of Lent—inviting us into "forty
days of tenderness." The contrast both with prevailing images
of Lenten asceticism and the norms of much of the environment created a juxtaposition that awakened us such that we
could meet God and each other anew.

The importance of this sort of sensitivity in the educational environment is apparent if we reflect on those moments
in which we have been dealt with tenderly. Is not the gift of
tenderness a consequent openness—that absence of defen-
siveness which is an essential condition for the most trans-
forming learning?

There is a third feature of the development of faith which
calls us to be tender. This is the recognition that with each new
development, with each new strength, there is a correspond-
ing new vulnerability. Piaget observed that the achievement of
the school age child is the development of the capacity for
"concrete operational thought." The younger child cannot

distinguish between dreams or nightmares and waking reality. The older child can make such distinctions, but is now vulnerable to an absolute literalism, not yet having the capacity for symbolic or abstract thought. For example, I have a friend who is now a Roman Catholic sister, who remembers when she was a child being told that when a bell rang at a certain time in the Mass, it was because Jesus had come to the Mass. She then remembers her devastation when one day she saw that the bell rang because one of the altar boys off in the wings was ringing it!

In the next era of development, adolescence, one can think symbolically and therefore is emancipated from concrete literalism, but there is, again, a new vulnerability. The capacity for "formal operational thought"—the capacity to think about thinking, to think abstractly—makes possible the achievement of what is termed "third person perspective taking."[9] With adolescence comes the ability to take the perspective of a third person, while still holding one's own perspective and that of another with whom one is interacting. But with this achievement of complex perspective taking (so essential for moral judgment) comes also a new self-consciousness. This was expressed most poignantly by a fifteen year old who shyly remarked, "I wonder what they are thinking about me, because I know what I am thinking about them."

In mid-life also there frequently emerges a new vulnerability which is particularly confounding because it may come in the midst of "success." One has built an "adult life" composed of significant responsibilities, commitments, and achievements. Yet the very strength one has achieved now makes it possible for whatever pain there is in one's past and whatever dreams and yearnings are yet unrealized to surface—demanding attention. The one who has "had it all together" now feels not so confident, not so peaceful, not so settled inside. To expose this sense of inner fragility and uneasiness to a public which assumes one to be strong and competent may feel discordant and seem to threaten the very ground of one's relationships, vocation and faith. But to attempt to ignore the inner movement of one's life and heart seems perilous as well. A person may feel that there is no place where both the truth of one's strength and the truth of a new bewildering vulnerability to the pain and promise of life may be received with both honor and tenderness.

If Yahweh remembers that we are dust, that growth costs, that we need each other, that even when we are strong we are also vulnerable—can we remember? Can we remember?

One day I was shopping in the supermarket, heard a crash, and turned around to discover that a young girl of about nine had managed on her way to the development of better coordination to cut a corner a bit too sharp and send four bottles of carefully displayed Perrier water into a mess of broken glass and water on the market floor. The store personnel quickly appeared with pails and mops, and, thankfully, also courtesy and kindness as the girl stood nearby with her mother, looking distressed and embarrassed. After all was cleaned up and the girl and her mother were left alone, I could see that the mother started to ask what happened, but before the girl could even begin to respond, the mother spontaneously put her arms around her daughter and gave her a warm hug.

Apparently I had recently spent too many counseling hours with too many folk who had not experienced that sort of acceptance from their parents, and I was touched and found it necessary to turn away and stare at a bin of cheese while I regained my composure. Later, I saw the mother in another part of the store and I stopped just long enough to tell her that I had seen her response to her daughter, and that as a psychologist and a theologian I wished that we had more mothers like her. What impressed me was that her immediate response was to say, "Oh, but it's so easy to remember."

Do we remember the vulnerability of the eras we have left behind? Dwayne Heubner has suggested that perhaps the most important use of faith development theory is that it can serve us as a "scaffolding of memory."[10] He asserts that the important matter is not to stand apart and interpret what another is experiencing through the lens of this theory, but, rather, to use this theory to help us interpret our relationship to another. What is now the character of our interaction? What do we mean to each other? The question is not "What stage are they in?" as much as it is "How shall we understand and fittingly meet the strength and vulnerability of the other?" Our response must be shaped by the other's experience of it. Descriptions of the stages or eras of human growth and development may serve us as a scaffolding of memory, inviting us to relationship, respect and tenderness.

But we have not yet said enough if we are to grasp adequately this admonition from Yahweh. If we practice only tenderness and compassion, we may fail to fulfill our vocation as faith educators, for we run the risk of losing our way in sentimentality and inappropriate affirmation.

When I was invited to speak on this subject, I had some suspicion that I had been assigned this particular part of this Scripture passage because I am the woman on the program. And then I wondered if I qualified for speaking to this subject, as I remembered that once when I was involved in a relationship in which issues of justice were at stake, a friend had remarked to me, about me, that he "had never seen anyone love so fiercely." At the time I had not been sure just how I should receive his meaning, for I was aware that fierceness can connote violence. Later, however, after some significant recomposing of his own life, with a sense of quiet affirmation, he shared with me that he had learned that he too could love fiercely. I knew then that he also was pointing toward that which we must recognize as a part of Yahweh's tender love. Let me explain more of what I mean.

I am not a Hebrew scholar, and dependent, therefore, upon my colleagues, I went in preparation for our reflection here to Paul Hanson, professor of Old Testament. I asked him if the full meaning of the words *ahab* and *hesed* is captured in the translation "to love tenderly." He considered this and said, "Yes, but the love referred to here is to be like Yahweh's covenant love, continually calling us into new and more faithful being; it is love that reaches out to us not only tenderly, but also tenaciously." According to the English dictionary, tenacious may mean "keeping a firm hold on life," and fierceness may mean "to be intensely determined." If we are to be faithful to our vocation to love as Yahweh loves, we are called, not only to be tender, but also to be intensely determined to hold firm to life—life in the sense of, "I have set before you on this day life and good, death and evil....Choose life."[11] This sense of life is recognized in right relation with God and with each other. Such life is characterized by a love that manifests itself, not in sentimentality, but in justice.

And now let us return for a moment to the story of the Perrier water, the girl, and her mother. I shared that same story in one of my classes, illustrating the same point—the importance of remembering the vulnerability of each era in life. However, after I had done so, one of my students, a black woman, asked the question, "But what if the girl and her mother were black and the market was in another part of the city, and the manager was not so understanding and insisted that the broken bottles were to be paid for, and the cost would consume the family's grocery money for a week? Perhaps the black mother would love her daughter just as much and remember just as clearly what it was to be nine years old, but in the midst of the financial anxiety, might she not yell at her daughter instead of hug her?"

As faith development theory is beginning to significantly influence pastoral-educational practice, describing stages of faith must not serve merely as a scaffolding of memory for white, middle and upper class experience. If a description of stages of faith is to serve our collective task, it must be appropriated, not only as a scaffolding of memory, but also as a scaffolding of promise and possibility for the whole human family. Piagetian psychology teaches us something about the development that is possible for a human life—but not inevitable. To take constructive-developmental theory seriously from the perspective of biblical faith is to recognize that there is no escape from the recognition that the fulfillment of the potential of each human life depends, in part, on our faithfulness—both individual and collective.

As suggested earlier, one of the most significant (and yet unrealized) aspects of a Piagetian paradigm is its power as a psychological model to compel our attention to sociological phenomena. Since persons develop not simply as an unfolding process from within but in dynamic interaction with their whole environment, we are compelled to recognize the dependence and inter-dependence of all life. Therefore, it is not enough that pastors and other educators be psychologically informed and respond individually to the individuals with whom we are in direct relation; we must also be sociologically aware and create the social structures which make possible the responses that lead out toward life for all. If all life is formed in inter-action, the whole fabric of life is our concern. We must not only know and understand persons but also the world that shapes them, and lead out in the transformation of both.

It is precisely this conviction that in every age has served to ground the most faithful practice of the people of God. Biblical faith witnesses to salvation not simply as individuals but as a people. The work of Thomas Groome is helping educators in this generation to remember that to be a Jewish or Chrisitan faith educator is to educate—to lead out—toward the kingdom or the commonwealth of God.[12] Values of the commonwealth of God—inclusion, justice, love, peace, and righteousness—stand in marked contrast to much that dominates our present historical context and shapes our suffering: the unqualified relativization of all authority, private interests, single issue politics, nationalistic machismo, consumer passion, and an attraction to the letter rather than the spirit of religious life.[13] Faithful leadership must be intensely determined to keep a firm hold on the purpose toward which we educate—a vision of the commonwealth of God. This is not to affirm a reactionary posture. Quite the contrary. To be engaged in the on-going life of faith is to expect that we are required over and over again to let go of finite forms and to participate in the on-going creation of a more obedient and faithful reflection of our covenant life with Yahweh.

Yahweh asks that we become again and again a people who embody an alternative imagination in the midst of and over against the prevailing, inadequate consciousness or conscious-less-ness of every age. Walter Brueggemann articulates this conviction in vivid images for us in his book *The Prophetic Imagination*.[14] Directing our attention to the story of Moses and the formation of Israel, he observes that what was happening in the story of the exodus was not simply the leading out of a band of slaves from bondage to freedom—as important as that is, especially if you are in that little band. Rather, Moses was posing an alternative consciousness to the royal consciousness.

There is always a "royal consciousness" which defends its finite form of life at the expense of the lives of others. If we are to educate toward the commonwealth of God, then we will as educators participate in the creation of communities which pose an alternative consciousness to that royal consciousness. And if they are to do so, they will serve as contexts of transformation, contexts which, while firm in purpose, are simultaneously tender in receiving the vulnerabilities of hurt and hope so as to nurture more faithful life. Such communities manifest their vocation by serving as *holding environments* in which life can come unraveled and be rewoven, as *communities of confirmation* which affirm new being, particularly in its initial and fragile forms (for both children and adults), but also as *communities of contradiction* which continually challenge the finite and idolatrous forms of faith, refusing to rest in forms which offer love and justice for some, but not for all.

Now let us return to the image of the six year old girl holding fast to the wedding ring of her foster mother. See her as an individual child with a particular history and potential. See her also as every child in our foster-care system for the children of vulnerable parents. See her dependence and vulnerability, but also see her fierce, tenacious hold on life. Does she not represent the vulnerability and the potential of the whole worldwide human family whom Yahweh loves and asks us to love?

And now I invite you to return in your mind's eye to the place of your daily ministry—your parish, home, agency, city or town. What does this little girl and all she represents need you—us—to be and become and do? What pain and hopes calls out for tenderness? In the place of your daily work, what are the structures of injustice that call for a fierce tenacious hold on a vision of the commonwealth of God—a hold that will not let go until justice flows down like a mighty stream?

What does Yahweh ask of us? Only this,

- to love tenderly,
- to love fiercely,
- to love tenaciously.

We are called to be tenderly and fiercely determined to hold firm to life—even as Yahweh holds us.

Notes

1. This story is told as I heard it from my father, Emmett F. Parks, a pastor who shared the story in the context of a sermon. The original story, "Someday, Maria," by Eddie Albert is published in *The Guideposts' Treasury of Love,* Carmel, New

York: Guideposts Associates, Inc., 1978, pp. 211-215.

2. For primary reference see James W. Fowler, *Stages in Faith: The Psychology of Human Development and the Quest for Meaning*, San Francisco: Harper & Row, 1981.

3. Jim Fowler and Sam Keen, *Life Maps: Conversations on the Journey of Faith*, ed. Jerome Berryman, Waco, Texas: Word Books, Publishers, 1978, p. 37.

4. Wilfred Cantwell Smith, *Faith and Belief*, Princeton, New Jersey: Princeton University Press, 1979, esp. chap. 6.

5. William F. Lynch, *Images of Faith: An Exploration of the Ironic Imagination*, Notre Dame: University of Notre Dame Press, p. 125.

6. Erik H. Erikson, *Childhood and Society*, Second Edition, New York: W.W. Norton & Co., 1950, pp. 247-251.

7. James W. Fowler, "Perspectives on the Family from the Standpoint of Faith Development Theory," *The Perkins School of Theology Journal* 23, no. 1 (Fall 1979), p. 31.

8. Robert Kegan, *The Evolving Self: Problem and Process in Human Development*, Cambridge, Massachusetts: Harvard University Press, 1982, pp. 115-116.

9. Robert L. Selman, *The Growth of Interpersonal Understanding: Developmental and Clinical Analyses*, Academic Press, 1980, pp. 102-105.

10. See "From Theory to Practice: Curriculum," Dwayne E. Huebner interviewed by William B. Kennedy, *Religious Education*, Vol 77, No. 4 (July-August 1982).

11. Dt 30:15 and 19.

12. Thomas H. Groome, *Christian Religious Education: Sharing Our Story and Vision*, San Francisco: Harper & Row, 1980.

13. Here I am indebted to Uri D. Herscher, "Future Tense: American Jews and Israelis," address presented at the Annual Meeting of the National Association of Jewish Educators, 1983.

14. Walter Brueggemann, *The Prophetic Imagination*, Philadelphia: Fortress Press, 1978.

THOMAS H. GROOME

Walking Humbly With Our God

Our assembly here is itself a sign of how we are to walk humbly, and together, with our God toward God's reign of love and justice. To my knowledge, this is the first time that all the mainline Christian churches, Catholic and Protestant, have joined together for a statewide convention of Christian educators. In this ecumenical action, we are being faithful to the ministry that is ours as educators in our Churches. We are attempting to lead out *(educare)* toward becoming a united assembly of "those who are called out" —the *ekkletoi*—which is the etymological root of our word "Church." Let our assembly and discourse together, then, be a sacrament of the Church we are called to become.

Sharon Parks indicated her suspicion that she may have been asked to speak about "loving tenderly" because she is a woman. I cannot, for the life of me, imagine why I was chosen to speak about humility—except that I have always been proud of mine.

The Question

"What's it all about?" is our colloquial way of asking an ultimate, perhaps *the* most basic human question. It has been asked, in one way or another, by every generation of the human family since the dawn of consciousness. It is the great "leveling" question that brings us to the foundations of our existence. From that bedrock, we have raised up our most elaborate philosophical and theological constructs to respond to it, knowing that if we cannot, then our lives are meaningless and we are absurd. Rahner would advise that we must raise such a question of ultimate meaning out of existential necessity. The very fact that we have the innate capacity for self-transcedence, the existential ability to reflect upon ourselves, means that we must inevitably ask the meaning of our lives.[1]

Our Western way of asking the ultimate meaning question is, however, distinctly Greek in its style. It presupposes that the meaning of life can be found in a metaphysics of life. The old Hebrews, on the other hand, were convinced that the meaning of life is found in how the community actually lives rather than in systems of philosophizing. That, I believe, is why Micah asks the ultimate meaning question as he does: "What does Yahweh ask of us?" However we live in response to that question will be the measure of meaning that we make out of life. And Micah gives the classic summary of what that response must be:

That we act justly,
love tenderly,
and walk humbly with our God (6:8).

As my colleagues have reflected on the first two lines of Micah's response, I will focus on the meaning of walking humbly with our God. My perspective throughout will be that of a Christian religious educator, my own ministry and alleged expertise. I will begin with a brief exegetical reflection on the passage itself to set the context for the body of the essay. (The more scholarly exegesis has already been done by our colleague Walter.) I will then raise up, as I see it, what it means for us Christians to "walk humbly with our God" and the implications of such a mandate for how we carry on the ministry of Christian religious education.

The Heart of the Matter

Micah, the last of the four great eighth century prophets (the others being Isaiah, Hosea and Amos), came from poor and oppressed farming stock in the little village of Moresheth, some twenty-five miles southwest of Jerusalem. He was influenced by Amos, possibly by Hosea, and it has been conjectured that he may have been one of Isaiah's disciples. It was probably his own roots, however, among the economically oppressed (as Brueggemann says "from below") that gave him his passion for social justice and his abhorrence of religious ritual while the demands of the covenant were being ignored. The demand for justice as the pre-condition for true worship of Yahweh is Micah's central theme.

Micah 6:8 is the climax of a passage that begins in 6:1. King sees the whole piece as "the Magna Carta of prophetic religion."[2] It is constructed as a covenant lawsuit that Yahweh brings against Israel, and indeed against all humanity (note: as the charge is presented it is clearly Israel that is on trial but at the punch line of 6:8 the one addressed is *Adam*—all humankind).

In verses 1-2, Yahweh summons Israel to stand trial. Yahweh is both judge and prosecutor. The mountains and foundations of the earth are God's witnesses. Israel stands accused of unfaithfulness.

In verses 3-4, the plaintiff Yahweh lays out God's charge by appealing, not to statutes written in law books, but to the memory of Israel. The people have forgotten the mighty saving deeds of God on their behalf; they have failed to remember how God freed them from the slavery of Egypt and brought them into this fair land, their inheritance.

In verses 6-7 we hear the defendant's feeble plea. But Israel has no case. Its very response shows how right the charge is, how much the people have forgotten. Israel implicitly recognizes its guilt and presumes that Yahweh wants a religious sacrifice in recompense. They ask: How great must the sacrifice be? Does Yahweh's wrath demand even the sacrifice of their first born? But that attitude is precisely Israel's sin. They have forgotten that religious sacrifice without living the justice, love and peace demanded by the covenant is a sham. This brings Yahweh to the indictment, for Yahweh has already shown Israel what is "good." Here the prophetic attorney gives us the classic summary of what Yahweh asks of all humankind. It is this, and "only this, to act justly, to love tenderly and to walk humbly with your God" (Mi 6:8). King writes: "This verse is a perfect summary of the teaching of the great eighth century prophets—Amos on righteousness (justice), Hosea on steadfast love, Isaiah on faith and obedience."[3] Anderson comments similarly: "Here we find, expressed in a single sentence, Amos' demand for justice, Hosea's appeal for the steadfast love that binds people in covenant with God and with one another, and Isaiah's plea for the quiet faith of the humble walk with God."[4]

Humble Walking

The last clause of Micah 6:8 should never be read without remembering the first two lines, and indeed their whole context within Micah and the eighth century prophetic literature. At first reading, it would appear that the first two mandates pertain to our treatment of other people while only the third refers to our relationship with God. In fact, as we will see, all three refer to our relationship with God and all three refer to our relationship with other people. In Yahweh's covenanted community, the measure of one relationship is the measure of the other.[5]

The Bible commentators seem to agree that humble walking with God is indeed a description of a life in faith. As people who presumptuously refer to our era as "post-Enlightenment," however, we must approach the word "faith" with great caution and not assume that our understanding corresponds to the biblical notion of faith.

Many scholars have pointed out the tendency of our "rationalist" time to equate faith with belief,[6] and belief with rational assent to particular propositions or doctrines.[7] The valiant efforts of Parks, Fowler, *et al.* notwithstanding, it will be a long time before popular consciousness returns to a more holistic understanding of faith—a lived activity of knowing, trusting and doing God's will.[8] The latter is the biblical notion of faith and the way of walking that Micah has in mind.

G. Ernest Wright, commenting on the biblical notion of faith, writes:

> Faith is not a series of propositions which are either believed or not believed. It is instead that trust in God which leads one to follow him in whatever situation one may find himself, a trust which waits on the Lord, even in times when one is fearful for his life.[9]

Biblical faith is a radical trust in God—even when one is afraid for one's life—that is lived as commitment to the covenant with Yahweh. This holistic understanding of faith is preeminent in Isaiah, who, as the scholars contend, was probably the footnote for Micah's own understanding.

A locus classicus for First Isaiah's understanding of faith is found in the report of his encounter with King Ahaz (Is 7:1-9) as the latter went out to inspect the city's water supply. At the time, the tiny kingdom of Judah was caught in a pincers of international conflict. On the one hand, Ahaz was faced with the imminent threat of the anti-Assyrian alliance between Aram and Israel, marching to depose him. On the other hand, he had the option of throwing in his lot with the Assyrians, and thus becoming their vassal, worshiping their gods and betraying the covenant with Yahweh.

The weak and vacillating Ahaz was to take the latter course. But while he is contemplating his options, he encounters Isaiah. Isaiah calls Ahaz to a radical trust in God as the only one who can save the nation. Isaiah is aware of the terror that besets Ahaz's heart—a fear for his life. "Take care and remain tranquil," he advises, "and do not fear; let not your courage fail…" (Is 7:4). Then he adds the classic lines, "Unless your faith is firm, you shall not be firm" (Is 7:9). Ahaz needs more than faith as a belief in propositions. Such would not hold him now in the terror of his heart.

Anderson, to bring out the play on words here, paraphrases Isaiah 7:9 thus:

If your faith is not sure (*ta'aminu*)
your throne will not be secure (*te'amenu*).[10]

"Sure" and "secure" both derive from the verb *'amen* meaning to be firm, and the causative form of the verb means to have faith, to trust.

But in whom is this trust to be placed? In whom is Ahaz to stand firm? Not in himself, not in the Assyrians, not in any earthly power or politics, but only in Yahweh God. In the midst of a faithless generation, one that grasps after straws rather than clinging to Yahweh, Isaiah says of himself: "I will trust in Yahweh" (8:17), for Yahweh is "the eternal rock" (26:4), "a stone that has been tested. A precious cornerstone is a sure foundation, he who puts his faith in it shall not be shaken" (Is 28:16).

The imagery that Isaiah's understanding of faith suggests is that of a mountain climber. Ahaz is like a man dangling on the side of a mountain with an enormous drop beneath him. Isaiah says to Ahaz and to us: Cling to Yahweh as your firm foothold on the mountainside of life. No one else can hold you fast in your terror of the drop beneath. Faith calls us to a relationship with God that is radical trust in the face of every danger. For

Isaiah, writes Anderson, "faith is absolute trust in and dependence upon God" which "demands a complete and firm commitment of one's whole being to God."[11]

To walk humbly with our God, then, means to cling to
God as the bedrock of our life, to ground one's self in Yahweh
as the only sure foothold, and no matter what precipice lies
beneath us to know that security is found only in God. What
then does such faithful walking, such a right relationship with
God, mean for our lives in Christian faith? I believe it calls us to
(1) recognize who our God is (who is God), (2) realize how
God is for us (who God is), and (3) comprehend who we are
as God's people.

Who Is Our God?

Our way of making meaning out of life is, implicitly at
least, a statement about who is our God. James Fowler, in his
investigation of the developmental structures of faith activity,
has found that people create worlds of meaning for themselves
within some "ultimate environment," an outer horizon within
and in relation to which a person makes meaning out of life.
That ultimate environment, claims Fowler, is shaped by some
"center of value" to which we commit ourselves and must
commit ourselves if our lives are to make sense at all.[12] In other
words, every attempt to live the meaning of our lives is, in the
last analysis, a statement about our ultimate center of value,
about who is our God. A prerequisite, then, for walking humbly
with our God is to realize who is God of our lives. Whoever it is
will shape our walking.

In asking, "Who is our God?" we are taking up a central
theme of the whole biblical tradition. The life history from
which the Hebrew Scriptures arose reflects a constant struggle
by the people of Israel to know and remain faithful to the God
of their lives. Their sin always stems from forgetting who is
their God and their salvation is found only by remembering

and returning to Yahweh, their one true God. They learned this lesson the hard way. Whenever they put their trust in themselves, in power, fortune, the neighboring gods, golden calfs, or whatever, they become lost; they return symbolically to the slavery of Egypt again. As long as they remember who is the God of their lives, they walk faithfully and humbly to their true identity as God's own free people. A summary statement of Hebrew faith might well be: "Let God be God."

Having learned from experience that they must allow no one and nothing to be God but Yahweh God, it is little wonder that they named the first law of the Decalogue as they did: "You shall not have other gods besides me" (Ex 20:3). In one sense, the nine commandments that follow are an exegesis of this first one. To live by the Decalogue means to keep only Yahweh as one's God. To break any one of the Decalogue is to forget who is God. Only with God as God could they find true freedom and salvation. Is this not what Jesus must have meant when John has him say "Eternal life is this: to know you, the only true God, and him whom you have sent, Jesus Christ" (Jn 17:3)?

In one way or another, sin always has its roots in some form of idolatry—turning away from God and placing someone or something else in God's place. While we have become more sophisticated in the kinds of idols that we make for ourselves (though gold is still a favorite), our struggle with idolatry is no less than it was for the Israelites. In fact, given the social and economic structures in which we dwell, the temptation to idolatry may be more compelling in our own age than at any other time in history.

John Francis Kavanaugh argues that the dominant mode of relating to life in this consumer culture is the "commodity form." In our form of culture we fetishize our commodities and give them a life of their own. Kavanaugh writes, "The commodity, like a god, achieves an independent existence over and against men and women." Then, "we begin to worship things as if they were persons, and we relate to other persons as if they were things."[13] He goes on to explain: "What Marx called the 'fetishism of commodities' is simply a form of idolatry in which human persons worship the products of their own hands."[14] The ultimate "God question" that we must ask ourselves, according to Kavanaugh, is: "What god do you believe in?"[15] In a culture where the things produced and consumed take primacy over the producers/consumers (we exist to produce/consume instead of producing/consuming to exist), it is counter-cultural to let God be our God. In a commodity form of culture, it is very difficult to avoid idolatry.

To walk humbly with our God means to place our trust only in God as the firm foothold that holds us on the mountain of life. That kind of conversion requires critical consciousness of how we fetishize our commodities and a spirit of relinquishment that is willing to "let go" of the false gods to which we cling.[16] The temptation to let something other than God be God is reflected in the temptation of Jesus in the desert. The wily tempter knew that only the greatest temptation might tempt a person like Jesus. According to Luke's account (Lk 4:1-13; see also Mt 4:1-11; Mk 1:12-13), the devil first tempted Jesus to turn stones into bread—a temptation to rely on his own powers as a source of life. Next Jesus was enticed with the power and glory of all the kingdoms of the earth—a temptation to make possessions and position the center of his life. The third temptation was to throw himself down from the pinnacle of the temple, thus putting God to the test—but in fact manipulating God to serve Jesus' own pretensions to greatness.

All three temptations were an attempt to get Jesus to place some one or thing other than the God he had come to know as Abba at the center of his life. Jesus' response to all three temptations was the same: I will let God be my God. If we are to walk humbly with our God, we too must resist the same temptations (only their forms change from age to age) to idolatry. We must let God—the God of Abraham and Sarah, the God of Jesus and Mary—be the God of our lives.

How God Is for Us

Beyond recognizing "who is our God," our humble walking also requires that we realize how God is for us—the kind of a God that we walk with.

In shifting from *who is God* to *how God is for us* I am attempting to focus on the image of God that we carry with us. Even those of us who claim to worship the one true God as the only God of our lives must still reflect on if and how our God is for us. Even as we say that we are ready to trust only in God, we need to know for what our God can be trusted. Conversely, if our image of God is a negative one, then we are not likely to trust in God for life.

The opening part of the passage in Micah, of which 6:8 is a climax, answers this question for us as adequately as any other part of the Hebrew Scriptures. There, before we hear what is asked of us, we read Yahweh's self-description: "I brought you up from the land of Egypt, and redeemed you from the house of bondage" (Mi 6:4). This is the kind of God that we have—a God who leads us out of slavery and brings us to freedom, a God who intervenes in history to bring us to fullness of life.

We remembered above that the first commandment of the Decalogue calls us to place God first in our lives, to let God be God. If we return now to its classic locations in the Scriptures, we notice that before the first commandment is named, Yahweh also gives a self-description of the kind of a God who is to be first in our lives. In Deuteronomy 5:6 and Exodus 20:2 we read: "I am the Lord your God, who brought you out of the land of Egypt, out of the house of bondage." Only when we know how God is for us is the first commandment stated. We can place God first in our lives, because our God can be trusted, even as only our God can be trusted, to bring us to life and freedom.[17] If we put any other god in God's place, then we are already on our way back to the slavery of Egypt. God asks of us what God asks of us because God wants us to be free.

When the Hebrews wanted to express their understanding of how God is for us, they often used the symbol of the reign of God. In the Hebrew Scriptures this is God's vision of peace and justice, freedom and wholeness (*shalom*) for all humankind. Jesus makes the coming of God's reign the raison d'etre of his own life. It is the central symbol of his word and work.[18]

With the kingdom as his purpose, and having been tested on who is his God, Jesus firmly placed a God of freedom at the center of his life. Immediately after his temptation, St. Luke's Gospel has Jesus come into the synagogue at Nazareth as the suffering servant in whom God's Spirit is working to fulfill the kingdom promise of Isaiah 61. Jesus now knows that God, his and ours, is a God who brings release to captives, sight to the blind, and liberty to those who are oppressed (see Lk 4:16-19).

In his short but classic work of more than twenty years ago, *Your God Is Too Small*, J.B. Phillips outlined some of the favorite false images of God that are prevalent even among those of us who claim to worship the one true God. He listed: God the resident policeman, the parental hangover, the grand old man, the managing director, the puppeteer, the god in a box, and many more. When our God is that small, then God too becomes a fetishized commodity, a product that we have made. Such false images of God are idols and idols always lead us back to Egypt again. The true God is one we can trust to lead us to life and freedom. That is who God is and how God is for us.

Who We Are as God's People

A constant thesis in the writings of Karl Rahner, and indeed of many other great theologians, is that a statement about God is also a statement about ourselves, and vice versa. If we know who is our God and how our God is, then we are well on our way to discerning our own identity. If God is our God, then we are God's people. If our God is a God of life and love, a God who wills freedom, justice and peace for all, then we must be a people who so live. What God wills to us becomes God's will for us. We must live according to what God intends for us and for all—we must do God's will. This means that to walk humbly with our kind of God, we must walk in solidarity with all people toward the values of God's reign. We must be for life, love, freedom, peace and justice because our God is for them. To the degree that we walk in death, hatred, oppression, violence, and injustice, or complicity thereto, the less we walk with this God that we claim to be ours.

This self-understanding is also evident in Micah's summary statement when we remember that the mandate to walk humbly with our God comes only after two previous mandates—to live justly and love tenderly. The third mandate has the first two as its pre-conditions and it is also their source of completion. When we live justly and love tenderly, we walk humbly with our God. Conversely, to walk humbly with our God means that we must live with love and justice toward all God's people.

The favorite Hebrew way of expressing their self-understanding in relationship to God was in terms of the covenant. It is important for our self-understanding to raise up the covenant imagery because it reminds us that as God's covenanted partners we are not reduced to passivity. Walking humbly with our God does not rob us of our responsibility, of our historical agency. The humility intended by such a covenant is far from a laissez faire attitude or a false humility that our efforts count for nothing. Such false humility lends itself to the heresy of what Bonhoeffer called "cheap grace." Far from robbing us of our historical agency, our covenant with God empowers our human responsibility and gives it its purpose. In partnership with God and each other, we are called to *walking*—not to passive standing still: to actively participate in the ongoing realization of God's reign.

To form ourselves and others in this kind of faith identity—a faith that is embodied in living for and by God's reign—is a most difficult task in our present social ethos. If our commodity culture makes it difficult for us to know who our God is, it makes it equally difficult for us to live as God's people. The basic operating principle of our social and political structures is competition rather than cooperation, individualism instead of solidarity, self-sufficiency instead of interdependence. To live our identity as God's people calls us to be counter-cultural, to swim against the tide of our ethos and transform it. Sponsoring ourselves and others to such identity in faith calls for a religious education that is more a process of subversion than of socialization, more consciousness raising than information imparting. We are now ready to reflect in detail on the implications of the above for the ministry of Christian religious education.

Education for Humble Walking

Education of any kind has four constitutive variables—the teacher, the students, the tradition of learning to be made accessible, and the history/world within which those three variables encounter each other. And religious education attends deliberately and explicitly to another constitutive variable—the reality of the Transcendent as the ultimate ground of being, the "other dimension." Christian religious education specifies this Transcendent dimension further to recognize the God revealed in the Hebrew and Christian traditions.

Having reflected above on who is our God, how our God is for us, and who we are as God's people, we will now reflect on how such a God and self-identity qualify the four constitutive variables in our educational ministry. To educate for walking humbly with such a God as ours, calls for a particular attitude toward ourselves and toward our students, and gives us specific responsibilities toward our Tradition and the world.

Ourselves as Teachers

All functions of Christian ministry are ways of representing Jesus Christ in service to the community for the building up of the body (see Eph 4:11-12). Let us reflect on what *representation* and *service* mean for the ministry of Christian religious educators.

Representation: to represent Jesus Christ means to act on his behalf. It does not mean to replace him or substitute for him.[20] He continues to be responsible for the process and we are no more than vessels of clay through whom he chooses to act.

This calls for a kind of humility in which we faithfully fulfill our responsibility for representation but do not present ourselves as "answer people." "Answer person" is indeed a traditional image of the teacher into which most of us have been socialized. To do Christian religious education as a representative of Jesus Christ calls for a dying to that old self-image and a conversion to another self-understanding as teacher.

If we present ourselves as "the answer person," in a sense we have forgotten who our God is and have assumed the trappings of divinity ourselves. This will bring people to us rather than to God in Jesus Christ. Ironically, there has been a strong assumption traditionally among Christian educators that we must have all the answers if we are to bring people to God. The fact is that people often come to God when we run out of answers. When we realize that the last question asked cannot be answered, people can come to dwell in mystery and encounter the presence of God.

Service: the call to service also points to the need for conversion on our part away from the traditional teacher image of "power over" toward a new self-image of "presence with."

Freire is correct when he claims that there is always a power dimension in any educational encounter. He makes the point that the teacher is the dominant holder of that power and can use his or her power as either "power over" or as "power with."[21] As educators we can use our power to control people or to empower people. If we remember the God with whom we walk together then, educating for such walking must be rendered through a service that is a "power with" people, a ministry that empowers all of us to embody and live God's word in humble walking. Our authority is no more than the right to serve (see Mk 10:45), and our service must be, by God's grace, one of empowerment.

This kind of "walking with" calls for a kenosis on our part, the kind of self-emptying that Paul attributes to the Christ, the one that we would represent (see Phil 2:5-7). We must die to the image of "teacher" into which we have typically been socialized and, without falling into false humility or abandoning our responsibility, come to see ourselves as fellow or sister pilgrims to the people with whom we walk. We are indeed guides to them in Christ's name, but it is our journey too. As we point ahead of them we also point ahead of ourselves. Rather than talking down to them from our hierarchical perch, there must be a leveling of the ground between us. We must walk together.

To live into that kind of identity as teachers requires that we attempt to embody the Word in our own lives. The Word made flesh in Jesus must constantly become flesh again in the lives of his followers, and especially in the lives of us who would represent him. As the Word made flesh to represent God, Jesus was "with us" to empower rather than "over us" to control. As Edward Powers said so well: "If it took God an incarnation to embody his message, we will not do it with less."[22]

Toward Our Students

As humble walking with God calls us into a new image of ourselves as teachers, so too it calls us to a new attitude toward students very different from the typical one. I wager that the dominant image conjured up by the word "student" in popular consciousness is of "dependent people" and "objects to be fashioned." Students are people that teachers either do things for or do things to (what Buber would call an I/It relationship). Indeed, sad to say, the language of behavioral objectives in some educational literature would seem to make the same assumptions.

In Christian religious education, the dependency assumption typically finds expression in the attitude that the teacher is the one who knows and communicates religious truths to the students who don't know them (what Freire calls "banking education"). The assumption that they are "objects to be fashioned" usually means trying to make good little Catholics, Baptists, Presbyterians, or whatever, in our own image and likeness. Both assumptions are antithetical to humble walking with God and educating others to so walk.

Rather than *"objects* to be made," our students are *subjects* in whose life God is already active and calling them to become their own unique selves. Instead of dependence, our students are called into interdependence with a community of faith in which they accept their responsibility for becoming makers of history—their own and the history of our world. They are not to be domesticated into our reality as it is— creatures of our world and Church—but have the vocation to be co-creators and re-creators of our common reality.

To honor them as subjects we must be with them in a way that brings them to speak their own word, to name their own reality and the presence of God therein, rather than to simply repeat our word or submit to what we know about God. They are to become "walkers with us" rather than people who fall in behind us. To honor their potential to be makers of history, we must be with them in a way that brings them to decision, their own decisions, in which they accept responsibility for living their faith by humble walking with our God together. (We will return to decision making again below.)

The God we worship as God's people calls us as teachers into partnership with our students, into a subject to subject relationship of mutuality and dialogue. Letty Russell contends that a constant purpose of Christian education is partnership, true koinonia, with each other in Jesus Christ. But if partnership is our purpose, then partnership must be our process as well. As Russell writes, "the purpose is also the method."[23] Such mutuality and partnership calls for a humility on our part by which we are truly open to hear the word of our students, to learn from them. We must be convinced that God is as capable of disclosing himself *to us* through them as *through us* to them. (How Sharon Parks learned from the reaction of her student to the food store incident is a good example of what I mean.) Only with such an attitude toward our students are we likely to walk humbly ourselves and sponsor our co-partners to walk together with our God.

Responsibility Toward the Tradition

To walk humbly with our God we must know the Story of those who walked the pilgrimage before us and now walk with us. While God is with us in our time and disclosing himself to us, we must also remember the Story of those before us and what they came to know from God's self-disclosure in their time. Without remembering that Story we will not know who we are or who we are called to become. On the other hand, in remembering the Story we find a symbol system to interpret and illumine our present, models of faith to live by, and liturgy to celebrate God's presence in our lives. When we reflect on the experiences of our lives in light of that Story we come to know for ourselves who is our God, how God is for us, and who we are as God's people.

By Story here I mean the whole faith Tradition (Scriptures, beliefs, rituals, sacraments, prayer forms, value systems, structures, expected life-styles, etc.) of the communion of saints, living and the living dead. That Story should be embodied faithfully in the present community of the body of Christ in the world, the Church. It is the task of educators within the community, however, to see to it that the Story is never forgotten. Our task is to make it accessible again and again to the present and rising generations.

We need to be careful as teachers not to impose our version of the Story on the participants as a hardened ideology. This is why I like the phrase "making the Tradition accessible."[24] It implies that the ones given access still retain their responsibility to do with it what they will as a living tradition of walking pilgrims. While we must faithfully remember where we have come from, the future of our community is not simply the repetition of our past. The Tradition is neither a negative control nor a limit upon our future but rather is the sustaining source from which we constantly draw new life.[25]

Giving access to the Tradition rather than imposing it upon people's lives means that the participants must be encouraged to critically appropriate the version of the Story that we make present. A critical appropriation of the Tradition requires questioning it, discerning its truth and its aberrations, coming to see it for ourselves, making it one's own. The Story is never information to be merely accepted. It is a faith Tradition to be acted upon, to be appropriated, recreated and integrated into one's own faith identity. Faithfulness to the Tradition demands such a critical appropriation of it.[26]

Responsibility to the World

To walk humbly with God is not to turn away from the world and fix our gaze on heaven. Our walking is with God in this world, which means, as Micah 6:8 would have it, walking with our neighbor in love and justice. We walk in a covenant that places the responsibility upon us of being faithful co-creators of God's reign in the world. Far from taking us away from the world, walking humbly with God brings us more deeply into it with a new sense of purpose—its transformation.

To highlight the responsibility for the world that humble walking with God places on us, let us recall Isaiah's understanding of faith that is so much at the heart of what Micah means by humble walking.

For Isaiah, the "acceptable sacrifice" that Yahweh expects from a life of faith is:

> To loose the bonds of wickedness,
> to undo the thongs of the yoke,
> to let the oppressed go free,
> and to break every yoke (Is 58:6).

James echos this understanding of faith when he writes: "Faith without works is dead" (Ja 2:26).

To educate people for humble walking is to sponsor them, by God's grace, to a faith that is done according to God's will for the world—the coming of God's reign.

Our educating for such faith must invite people to decision and the response of a lived Christian faith. That is what Jesus constantly invited from his hearers. So often, however, our curricula would seem to settle for people knowing about God's self-disclosure, or, at best, coming to an expression of thanksgiving for God's goodness to us who are sinners. Such knowing and praying are essential to our purpose, but if we are to walk humbly with this God of ours, then we must also accept our responsibility and historical agency toward the transformation of our society and world.

Lived faith in the world calls us to continually recreate the forms of our social, political, cultural and economic life and to build social and ecclesial structures that are more capable of promoting the values of God's reign. Educating for this kind of social responsibility in the world will require that we bring ourselves and others to question the present social structures and arrangements of our reality. We must educate for critical consciousness. By critical consciousness I mean the ability to see through and beyond the appearances of present reality that society asks us to take for granted. Our critical consciousness must cause a transformation in us that is lived in the context of social trasformation.

Conclusion: "Too Much"?

What Yahweh asks of us will always pose a huge challenge to all Christians and a large task for Christian religious educators. Micah 6:8 states it well for us, and we must not underrate the demands of the covenant. On the other hand, if we overrate the importance of our ministry as Christian educators to the point of feeling overwhelmed by it, then we have already missed the point of what it means to walk humbly with our God. When we take too much responsibility for the outcome, we are already forgetting who and how our God is and who we are as God's people. Our task is not "too much" if we remember that our God is still God, and a trustworthy One. Then, even as we accept responsibility for the task, we can continue to walk humbly together and know that the outcome of our efforts is not our own doing. It is always God's gift (see Eph 2:8).

Notes

1. See Karl Rahner, *Foundations of Christian Faith* (New York: Seabury Press, 1978), esp. Ch. 1.
2. Philip J. King, "Micah," in *The Jerome Biblical Commentary* (New Jersey: Prentice-Hall, Inc.) 1968, Vol. 1, p. 288.

3. *Ibid.*

4. Bernhard W. Anderson, *Understanding The Old Testament* (New Jersey: Prentice-Hall, Inc.), 1975, Third Edition, p. 318.

5. For this insight, I am indebted to my colleague Philip King, Professor of Old Testament, Boston College.

6. See Wilfred Cantwell Smith, *The Meaning and End of Religion* (New York: Harper & Row, 1978).

7. See Avery Dulles, "The Meaning of Faith Considered in Relationship to Justice," in *The Faith That Does Justice,* John C. Haughey, ed. (New York: Paulist Press, 1977).

8. I have written in more detail elsewhere about such an understanding of faith. See Groome, *Christian Religious Education: Sharing Our Story and Vision* (San Francisco: Harper & Row, 1980), esp. Ch. 5.

9. G. Ernest Wright, and Reginald H. Fuller, *The Book of the Acts of God* (Garden City, N.Y.: Doubleday, 1960), p. 68.

10. Anderson, p. 310.

11. *Ibid.*

12. See James W. Fowler, *Stages of Faith* (San Francisco: Harper and Row, 1981), esp. Ch. 3.

13. John Francis Kavanaugh, *Following Christ in a Consumer Society* (Maryknoll, New York: Orbis Books, 1982), p. 6.

14. *Ibid.,* p. 11.

15. *Ibid,* p. 15.

16. See Maria Augusta Neal, *A Socio-Theology of Letting Go* (New York: Paulist Press, 1979).

17. It is unfortunate that when we teach the Decalogue in religious education we invariably begin with Exodus 20:3 or Deuteronomy 5:7—the first commandment—and forget the introductory verse that portrays Yahweh as a liberating God. Perhaps this is why Christians so often see the commandments as negative curtailments upon our lives. In fact, they are guidelines to us from a God of freedom on how we can remain free.

18. For an overview of the kingdom of God in Scripture and its implications for religious education, see Groome, *op. cit.,* Ch. 3.

19. See J.B. Phillips, *Your God Is Too Small,* (New York: Macmillan, 1961).

20. Dorothea Soelle, *Christ the Representative* (Philadelphia, Fortress Press, 1967).

21. See Paulo Freire, *Pedagogy of the Oppressed* (New York: Seabury, 1970), pp. 126ff.

22. Edward A. Powers, "On Keeping One's Balance," in *A Colloquy on Christian Education,* John H. Westerhoff, ed., (Philadelphia: United Church Press, 1972), p. 58.

23. Letty Russell, *Growth in Partnership* (Philadelphia: Westminster, 1981), p. 49.

24. For this image of "making accessible" in talking about the tradition, I am indebted to my colleague Mary C. Boys. Boys writes: "My claim is that 'make accessible' is the verb which ought to function as the primary description of religious education." "Access to Traditions and Transformation," in *Tradition and Transformation in Religious Education,* Padraic O'Hare, ed. (Birmingham, Alabama: Religious Education Press, 1979), p. 15.

25. One of the arguments against ordination of women offered in official statements by the Roman Catholic Church is that such a practice is contrary to the Tradition. To use Tradition that way on such a question is to presume that there can be nothing in our future unless it was in our past. That is a misunderstanding of the role the Tradition plays in the faith community.

26. For a more detailed statement on critical appropriation see Groome, *op. cit.,* pp. 195-197 and 217-220.

TO ACT JUSTLY, LOVE TENDERLY, WALK HUMBLY

The Prophet Micah long ago laid down a guideline for authentic religious behavior when he said: "This is what Yahweh asks of you, only this: To act justly, to love tenderly, and to walk humbly with your God."

These criteria can assist believers—and especially ministers—in today's church, for they provide a convergent point for praxis and spirituality. In this book an Old Testament scholar, a psychologist and a religious educator have come together to reflect on the three elements of the text. Individually they ask: How do the scriptures require us to respond to the problems of a real world? How can we maintain love in our ministrations to others? How can we speak with real authority while still keeping our humility?

Walter Brueggemann is Senior Professor of Old Testament Studies at Eden Theological Seminary in St. Louis, Mo.

Sharon Parks is Associate Professor of Religion and Psychology at Harvard Divinity School, Cambridge, Mass.

Thomas H. Groome is Associate Professor of Theology and Religious Education at Boston College, Chestnut Hill, Mass.

Paulist Press
0-8091-2760-1

Cover design: Moe Be